New York and Los Angeles City Guide

A Complete Guide to Discover and Know the Best of the East Coast and the West Cost of the United States

By

Easton Lincoln

Respective authors own all copyrights not held by the publisher.

The information herein is offered for informational purposes solely and is universal as so. The presentation of the information is without contract or any type of guarantee assurance.

The trademarks that are used are without any consent, and the publication of the trademark is without permission or backing by the trademark owner. All trademarks and brands within this book are for clarifying purposes only and are owned by the owners themselves, not affiliated with this document.

Table of Content

Guide 1

New York City

Guide

A Guidebook with Everything You Need to Know
To Explore New York's Beautiful Places.

Introduction

Despite the fact that there are hundreds of cities around the world, some stick out like others, rising to the top of the many possible options and acquiring a reputation as something truly distinctive. This is especially true when considering New York Metropolis, a city so well-known that it goes by multiple names (such "A Big Apple" and "The City That Never Sleeps") and even the moniker New York. Many individuals in that city may believe the word "city" is being used, and the word "state" must be added to refer to the state in which the city is located.

Whether you call it by that name or not, there's no disputing that New York City, whether you live there or are just passing through, is a very unique place. The fact that New York City is divided into five boroughs, each with its own borders, is possibly the most notable aspect. The borders were initially their counties, but as New York City grew, all of the county chairs and small-town governments were disbanded, and the city took on its current shape.

Each borough, on the other hand, is distinct, with a wide range of cultures and communities.

The following are the five boroughs of New York City:

- Brooklyn is a New York City borough.

- The Bronx is a New York City borough.

- Manhattan is a New York City borough.

- Queens are the world's most powerful women.

- Staten Island is a small island located off the coast of New York City.

Any of them might be used as a travel guide, and several of them are distinctive enough to be recognised even by tourists from afar, but nothing compares to how they come together to create a really unique city. NYC is on the list of fantastic cities not just because it is one of the world's largest and most populous cities, but also because there is so much to see and do everywhere you go.

Manhattan is known for its luxurious hotels, world-class shopping, and, of course, Wall Street and the financial district. The amount of money that passes through that part of town, as well as the sheer variety of pleasures available there, from high-end shopping to vintage corner shops, is almost unfathomable.

Brooklyn's modern renaissance has not gone unnoticed. Anyone familiar with hipster culture is aware of the massive creative reconstruction and revitalization that is taking place in vast parts of Brooklyn, a movement that is still fighting to retain the old school charm. As a result, lovely mixed-income neighbourhoods form, where blue-collar labourers and creative artists coexist.

Despite being surrounded by such an urban behemoth, the Statue of Liberty on Ellis Island is still one of the world's most recognisable symbols, and Central Park is only one of many parks across the city that allow visitors to get away from it all.

New York's nightlife is renowned, as the motto "The City That Never Sleeps" suggests, with everything from pubs and clubs to the infamous (or notorious, depending on your point of view) Red Light District. Anyone who has ever watched television on New Year's Eve, possibly while enjoying a home party, has seen the images of a million citizens in Times Square counting down to the New Year as a renowned lit ball descends in the final minute, culminating in cheers at the final countdown.

In terms of things to do and see, New York City has a lot to offer. Many of the world's best museums, libraries, and historical sites may be found here, while visitors will discover tucked-away businesses, lovely bars and restaurants, and far too many gems to list on every side of the city.

Take in a Broadway or off-Broadway show. Whatever a person's idea of a spectacular vacation or adventure is, it may be found in New York City. Whether you've lived in Fresh York for a long time or are a first-time visitor, you'll find something new to do and see when you go there, which is what makes it so special.

Chapter 1: Experience New York city

It's OK to visit the Giant Sea Way and eat your fill on New York pizza, but is it getting the most out of your stay in the city? Forget the Brooklyn Bridge trip at your next journey are 15 things you must do in New York City on your bucket list.

Attend a taping of a Television program as a member of the audience.

Snag a seat at the television show taping during your visit to one of the world's most screen-famous cities. Watch live tapings of shows including "Saturday Night, The Late Show featuring Stephen Colbert, Midnight starring Seth Meyers, & Good Morning America for free.

1.1 In Harlem, eat a chopped cheese.

The chopped cheese is a hyper-local tradition that is the half cheeseburger, half sandwich, and utterly amazing. Ground beef and American cheese, lettuce, and onions on even a pressed hero are the perfect snack after such a night of partying and can be found at every Harlem bodega.

1.2 Join tens of thousands of New Yorkers for such a mass movie screening.

Even on movie night, you wouldn't be able to keep New Yorkers inside in the summer. Summer city slickers must try picnicking at an outside screening event (they're BYOB!), such as Summer Screen, HBO Bryant Campground Camp Festival, & several others.

1.3 Look for that famous coffee cup.

You've seen it in the hands of your favorite fictional New Yorkers over decades—that ubiquitous blue & white paper cup. Finding a genuine Anthora cup is a treasured city experience. This icon of New York's famous on-the-go lifestyle has inspired innumerable copycats. Tip: Look for just an image of the amphora with the words "WE ARE HAPPY WIll SERVE YOU" next to it. Good luck with your search!

1.4 At Comedy Cellar, expect a surprise celebrity guest.

This renowned Greenwich Village comedy festival provides more than just laughter. Comedy Corner has hosted surprise acts such as Aziz Ansari, Dave Chappelle, Jon Stewart, & Jerry Seinfeld and is a frequent choice for top talent working out new material. Though you won't be able to plan for this, you'll be able to firmly call yourself a real New Yorker if it happens to you.

1.5 Take a trip to the beach.

Unfortunately, most people (including the many New Yorkers!) believe that there is no possibility to experience sand and sea vibes in the city. Join New Yorkers only at the city's many beaches, such as Fort Tilden, People's Beach, and Rockaway Beach, this summer.

1.6 At Grand Central Terminal, meet someone who is "on the clock."

Only a few things can draw folks to Midtown, including this world-famous monument. For millennia, making rendezvous plans that include the phrase "meet me under the clock" has been a timeless right of passage in New York.

1.7 At Marie's Crisis, join in a sing-along with strangers.

You don't have to be a musical theatre fan (while many customers are) to enjoy Marie's Crisis' famed show tune sing-alongs. This 128-year-old jazz club downtown Greenwich Village is indeed the best New York destination you've ever heard of, popular with LGBT locals and theatre performers.

Chapter: 2 City Tour

New York, one of the world's finest cities, is constantly a frenzy of activity, featuring famous sights around every corner and seldom enough time to have them all. Some tourists come to see the Broadway performances; others come to shop and eat; and still more come to view the sights, like the Lincoln Memorial, the Empire State Building, the Central Park, historic districts, Brooklyn Bridge, and countless world-renowned museums.

Many of the top spots to see in New York are within walking distance of one another or only a short train journey away, making touring a breeze in this city.

The High Line & One World Observatory, two newer tourist attractions in New York that opened in recent years, provide distinctive viewpoints of the city. There is always something to see & do in New York, no matter what time of year it is or what time of day and the night it is.

Even if the city doesn't have its normal high-energy feeling this year, that doesn't mean people shouldn't go. The city has become a different place due to the lower number of tourists, making it less expensive to explore & easier to explore, with shorter lines at popular attractions. You might want to take advantage of having the city to yourself. Our guide to New York's major attractions will help you plan your vacation.

2.1 The Statue of Liberty is the most famous monument in the United States.

The Statue of Liberty, America's most famous sight, has been at the top of every 1st tourist's list of stuff to do in New York. It was France's present to the United States. It is a universal emblem of freedom and one of America's greatest attractions, built-in 1886.

It is just over 152 feet tall at the base to torch and weighs around 450,000 pounds, making it one of the world's tallest monuments.

2.2 Central Park

A stroll, pedal, or float trip through Central Park's crisscrossing pathways is a must-do on anybody's New York City bucket list. You can even keep wearing your skates &

glide across Wollman Arena in the winter. One thing that makes New York such a lovely and pleasant city is this massive park inside the city center, a half-mile broad and 2.5 miles long.

2.3 Rockefeller Center and the Observation Deck at the Top of the Rock

Rockefeller Center will be on practically every tourist's itinerary when it comes to Future York attractions. The 70-story /30 Rockefeller Square, an Art Nouveau skyscraper with amazing views of Manhattan from the famed Top of the Rock Viewing Platform, is the centerpiece of this large entertainment & shopping area in the heart of Manhattan, which is home to NBC-TV as well as other media.

2.4 The Art Museum

A Metropolitan Art museum, often simply the Met, was established in 1870 and is among the most well-known museums inside the United States. The Metropolitan Museum of Art's permanent collection has about two million items of art spanning 5,000 years.

A Met Fifth Avenue is the museum's focal point, although it has three locations. American ornamental arts, arms and armor, Egyptian art, costumes, musical instruments, pictures, and much more are among the collection's highlights.

2.5 The Theater District and Broadway

One of the most popular things to see in Nyc is to see a Broadway performance. This is the spot to view the most recent plays and long-running classics, as it is regarded as the apex of American theatre.

The term "Broadway theatre" is commonly used to refer to many theatre facilities in the Entertainment District & along Broadway itself. Tickets with the most popular concerts should be booked in advance.

2.6 Empire State Building,

Empire State Building has been a good landmark and popular tourist attraction in New York City. Till the 1 World Trade Center skyscraper rose taller 41 years later, the 381-meter-tall, the 102-story structure was the world's tallest. When it first opened in 1931, the Empire State Building, which was topped with an airship mooring tower, became a landmark & a symbol for New York City.

An Empire State Building has two observatories, both of which offer spectacular views. On bright days, you could see up to 80 miles into Pennsylvania, New Jersey, Connecticut, & Massachusetts, which are all neighboring states.

2.7 The 9/11 Memorial & Museum

The twin 110-story World Trade Center towers previously ruled the Manhattan skyline before being demolished by homicide jetliners on September 11, 2001, resulting in a sad loss of life. Two one-acre square reflecting ponds have been built where the World Trade Center's two towers once stood.

The National September 11 Memorial pays honor to the nearly 3,000 individuals who died in the September 11, 2001, terrorist attacks, as well as the six individuals murdered in the previous Trade Center bomb in Feb 1993.

2.8 Times Square

Times Square, which is lined with massive, brightly illuminated billboards and displays, has been the place to be in Nyc at night, but it's also fascinating at any time day and. New York's New Years' celebrations occur here, including the famed "ball drop" at midnight when the square & surrounding streets are packed with people.

2,9 Brooklyn Bridge

The Brooklyn Bridge is among the city's most famous monuments, including its Gothic-shaped arch and suspension cables inspiring generations of poets, musicians, and painters. This historic bridge, which connects Manhattan and Brooklyn across the East River, was the world's largest first steel road bridge when it opened in 1883.

2.10 Fifth Avenue

Fifth Avenue is one of America's most famous shopping streets, and it is home to several of the world's most well-known designers' flagship businesses. This upscale boulevard is lined with Cartier, Bergdorf-Goodman,

Tiffany, the iconic iPhone Fifth Avenue, & of course, Saks Fifth Avenue, among many others.

A stroll down Fifth Avenue is enjoyable for shoppers and non-shoppers alike. The ideal region is between 60th Street & 40th Street, which runs roughly from the southern shore of Central Park to a Public Library.

Chapter 3: Shop In New York

As the United States' fashion center, New York City is in a class of its own and, making it simple to leave with a lighter wallet than when you arrived.

The question isn't so much what you'll buy as it is where you'll buy it. 5th Avenue is terrific location to start if you enjoy window shopping & spending a lot of money. You'll find high brow window displays and top-name designers eager to be astonished at.

There are plenty of one-of-a-kind shops and adorable boutiques to keep you busy for days if you heading toward south to Nolita (north of Little Italy) & roll yours shopping journey into Soho. If you want something a little different, cross the Williamsburg Bridge till this hipster enclave, where you browse cheese shops, antique boutiques and grab a cup of coffee mug at one of the many local cafés.

3.1 WILLIAMSBURG, N.C.

Even though Brooklyn & Manhattan were originally pitted against one other, Brooklyn have been gradually pushed the island away and seized the label of "cool." The streets of Williamsburg are extremely hip and stylish, with an astounding collection of street paintings & art. Hipsters congregate here.whether they're writing a song in hip cafe or perusing flea markets & food bazaar. for inspiration. Even Manhattanites must acknowledge that visiting Brooklyn for antique apparel or local independent boutiques is worthwhile. Ignore the chains & trying something new, such as Desert Island, which is a must-see for every comic book fan.

3.2 DISTRICT OF MEATPACKING

With a name like Meatpacking District, it's a surprise that this New York neighborhood has become a fashionable destination. This area, which was once the meat industry's headquarters, has been substantially altered (but former meat lockers and meatpackers remain). The high-tech Apple Store, located on Ninth Avenue and 14th Street, is crowded at all hours of the day and night. The hottest designer boutiques, including Jeffrey, Stella McCartney, and Catherine Malandrino, are located on the cobblestone streets. You'll also find the coolest hotels and amazing restaurants here. The Meatpacking District has something for everyone, whether you're a fashionista or a foodie.

3.3 NOLITAN

Thousands of immigrants flocked to New York for a better life, and NoLita (North of Little Italy) was formerly their home base. The streets are stylish and incredibly fashionable, with one-of-a-kind boutiques, shoe stores, jewelry vendors, and quirky downtown style setters. Unique things that will add flair to any wardrobe may be found in artist-driven boutiques, which are a joy to browse or purchase. NoLita is the uncommon mixture of trendy and friendly, from socially conscious children's apparel to thrift shop gems. Narrow streets are charmingly old-fashioned, and they're perfect for people-watching from one of the many independent cafes.

3.4 AVENUE MADISON

Tom Ford, Calvin Klein, Giorgio Armani, Luca Luca, Hermes, Carolina Herrara, and practically every high fashion designer can be found on Madison Avenue from 59th street through the 1990s. Hotels such as the Mark, Pierre, and Carlyle, frequented by celebrities and other dignitaries, are ultra-luxurious. It has become just as well known for its luxury and unrivaled shopping choices as it was once for the Nyc ad industry. The Whitney Museum and several art galleries are just an art beloved's dream. Outdoor cafes abound, and the jet-set frequent them for lunch in between spa & salon visits. Because here is where celebs shop, you will see them. Outside of Barney's, look again for limo & driver.

3.5 SOHO (South of the Highway) (SOUTH OF HOUSTON)

SoHo is formerly home to many New York manufacturers, including everything from tailoring to iron foundries & all in between. The warehouse buildings were all turned into loft spaces for elegant (read: costly) living, while for the rest of us, there are a plethora of high-end boutiques, shops, and stylish eateries. Between the Hollisters, H&Ms, and Zaras of the streets, you'll discover a branch of a Bloomingdales, Guggenheim Museum, even a Chanel boutique. You might easily spend a whole day walking the cobbled streets, pausing for food or a cocktail, and, of course, shopping.

3.6 FIFTH AVENUE is a street in New York City.

For a long time, Fifth Avenue has always been the core of New York's retail sophistication. Fifth Avenue, which runs between 39th & 60th Streets, is a must-see for every fashionista. Begin your shopping spree at Saks 5th Avenue & moving up to Bergdorf Goodman. Across the Street is a different store dedicated solely to guys. Cartier, Van Cleef and or Arpels, DeBeers, Harry Winston, and Tiffany's are among the stores along the path so you can window shop at your heart's content. Don't overlook St. Patrick's Cathedral & other magnificent churches, which sit beside businesses such as Louis Vuitton, Gucci, and Prada, all of which sell the world's finest goods.

3.7 SQUARE OF UNION

Union Square is the historic junction where Broadway & the former Bowery Road met in the early nineteenth century. It's now a massive shopping district with everything from Fresh Foods to Nordstrom Rack. It's especially charming during the holidays, with outdoor tents selling various presents, homemade soaps, scarves, and crafts. Union Square is home to the Greenmarket, where New York farms display local, organic, and fresh food & flowers in an outdoor setting on Mondays, Wednesdays, Fridays, and Saturdays. Because NYU is close by, students prefer cozy coffee shops like Think Coffee. Many of the city's best restaurants are also located here, including the freshly reopened Union Square Café, which has relocated a few streets up to 19th Street.

Chapter 4: Entertainment In New York

It is said that this is the city that never sleeps. New York City is without a doubt one of the world's most popular tourist attractions. Respectively during the day & at night, there is enough to do and see. Fortunately, several big attractions have extended hours. As a result, you'll be able to partake in some of the city's most exciting nighttime activities.

4.1 Dinner Cruise in New York

Enjoy a luxury evening out on one of New York's dinner cruises, such as the Bateaux, which includes a four-course delicious meal, entertainment, and spectacular views of the city. As you cruise through the lower half of Manhattan, take sights like the Chrysler Building, the Empire State Building, Statue of Liberty, and Brooklyn Bridge. Take in the intimate ambiance of your yacht, which, unlike larger boats, has superb views from nearly every table. Upgrade to an open bar to enhance your dining experience.

4.2 Helicopter Tour of Nyc

On an amazing 15-minute helicopter trip, see New York's major sights from the air. As you hover above the Hudson River, you'll come face to face with the Statue of Liberty. Admire the Empire State Building, Chrysler Building's glittering Art Deco brightness, and Central Park's sweeping green sweep. For any traveler to New York City, this is a must-see!

You'll see Manhattan's famed skyline in such a way that's difficult to see from the ground during this 15-minute New York tour helicopter flight. You'll also get a bird's eye view of America's most iconic icon, the Statue of Liberty!

4.3 The Falls of Niagara Plane Bateaux Day Trip from Nyc Dinner Cruise in New York

Almost certain to sell out! Enjoy gourmet meals and live jazz music while taking in stunning views of Manhattan, New Jersey, & Brooklyn skylines on this luxury Nyc dinner cruise. Battery Park, The Empire State Building, the South Street Seaport, the Statue of Liberty, and other sights can be seen from the viewing deck or the all-glass-covered cabin, providing breathtaking vistas at every turn. Upgrade to a first-class or romantic VIP experience that includes a personal table & French sparkling champagne!

4.4 Attend a Broadway performance.

There are more enjoyable things to do in Nyc at night, such as seeing a Broadway show. On Broadway in Nyc, you can be sure to see the top musicals and shows in the world.

It's a fantastic idea for amazing entertainment in one of the city's most interesting places. So, after soaking up all the adrenaline at Times Square, please ensure to see one of the numerous Broadway shows.

4.5 Spend some time in the Lower East Side.

Having a night out on Eastside is a beautiful image if you're searching for excellent pubs & restaurants in NYC, and it's one of my favorite free activities in New York in the evening whenever it finally goes out again to dance and for drinks.

After a certain hour, most places transform into a club and offer a very exclusive, local feel. It's also one of the more affordable places to go out dancing and drinking, and it's a wonderful nighttime activity in New It may be one of the much more affordable places to go dancing & drinking, and it's a wonderful nighttime activity in New York.

4.6 House of Yes

It is the most outrageous and entertaining nightlife in New York. Circus events, immersive movies, burlesque & cabaret performances, aerial extravaganzas, nightly parties, morning raves, BBQs, & bubble baths are all available at HOY.

Spending the night in House of Yes downtown Bushwick that's like entering up an entirely new world where sexual freedom reigns supreme. The transforming themed sets have an adult playground sense to them.

4.7 Attend a sport in New York City.

Whichever sport you enjoy, there is always something going on in Nyc when this comes to sports.

Catching a basketball, baseball, or hockey game is usually a good choice as one of my favorite fun night activities in NYC. Because there are ten largest sports teams in 5 different sports all situated in the city, there will almost certainly be a game going on throughout your visit.

4.8 Attend a comedy show to hone your giggling skills.

What could be more entertaining than witnessing a comedy concert in New York City? Some well comedic clubs (Comedy Cellar, UCB, etc.) and well-known comedians can be found in New York. What's my go-to? The Magnet Theatre in Chelsea is a must-see! This little improv club is just the greatest, in my opinion! On a Friday night, if you'd like to check it out, go there. The Friday Evening Show and Premiere: A Musical are two options. Both of these shows are fantastic. Other days are enjoyable as well, but nothing beats Friday Night. Tickets are only $10 per concert that night, which is a great deal.

4.9 Immerse yourself in the National Geographic Encounter.

The National Geographic Encounter's Ocean Odyssey is another multimedia, immersive experience in Nyc that is well worth your time! It will lead you through an underwater adventure where you will be able to see some of nature's most amazing species and wonders. There's no need to wear a bathing suit! It was fantastic, we all agreed.

4.10 At Gayle's Broadway Ros, you can listen to Broadway music.

I always recommend that restaurant to anybody searching for something exciting to do in NYC. In May of this year, New York will be home to another entertaining adventure. At Gayle's Broadway Rose, located in Midtown Manhattan, waiters and servers will sing Broadway music from you while you eat wonderful meals and some of the city's best milkshakes.

Chapter 5: Eat At New York

One of the best things about Nyc was its diversity of its people, and there's no smarter method to get a taste of the city's melting pot than through its cuisine.

If you enjoy eating, this list of the greatest restaurants in New York City is for you.

5.1 Katz's Delicatessen (Katz's Delicatessen)

Arguably one of New York City's most famous restaurants, Katz's Delicatessen has been serving iconic sandwiches since 1888.

The pastrami at Katz's Deli is the only reason anyone should eat there, even though they have a diverse menu. The pastrami is incredible, with a great fat-to-meat ratio & a topping of black pepper & secret spices. It's fall-apart tender. It's everything you'd want in a pastrami sandwich.

5.2 Pizza by Di Fara

Pizza is arguably among the first items that come to mind when thinking about cuisine in New York City; not eating pizza around NYC is like getting in the car & not driving anywhere - you do not do that.

You'll find hundreds of iconic pizza restaurants in every Nyc travel or food book, including Lombardi's, one of America's original pizzerias, and Grimaldi's, which is famed for its coal conveyor oven pizza.

5.3 The Halal Experts

What could be better than chicken and rice?

That was my thought before dining just At Halal Guys, among the first street food carts in New York City. Their cuisine is Middle-Eastern in origin, and they offer Halal meals, as their name implies.

Many individuals informed me about dining at The Halal Guys, "Ensure you get a lot more sauce, that both white and red chilli sauce."

5.4 Daughters of Russ

Russ and Daughters, a deli that began as a food stall pushcart & has been "Appetizing since 1914," is another Nyc landmark.

Russ and Daughters is a well-known Nyc restaurant specializing in smoked and salt-cured salmon served with bagels & cream cheese. They also provide various other delectable delicacies, such as herring, salads, & dried fruits & nuts.

5.5 Shake Shack is a restaurant that serves burgers and shakes.

Burger battles rage across the United States, from The into Five Guys.

New York's Shake Shack has been spearheading a burger revolution & wowing burger fans recently when it comes to the greatest burger chain in the US. Serious Eats has a comprehensive, fast-food chain taste test comparison.

5.6 Gloria's Caribbean Cuisine is a restaurant that serves Caribbean cuisine.

In Park Slope, Brooklyn, Gloria's Caribbean Cuisine offers a variety of Caribbean

dishes, most of which are Trinidadian in origin.

Gloria's Caribbean Cuisine is among the restaurants in NY you don't want to miss if you're looking for great curries and pleasant service.

5.7 Famous Foods of Xi'an

Xi'an Famous Foods, which has many shops throughout New York City, specializes in providing cuisines from Xi'an, a city in China's northwest.

Unlike Chinese Cantonese cuisine, Xi'an cuisine uses more spices, such as cumin, chilies (with plenty of chile oil), & Sichuan pepper.

5.8 No. 1 Tacos Los Tacos

Los Tacos No.1 can satisfy any need if you're seeking some of the best tacos Nyc has to offer, and maybe as delicious as tacos somewhere else in the United States.

You can now choose between corn and flour tortillas for your tacos. You may top the tacos with cilantro, onions, & guacamole, as well as salsa, more dry chiles, and lime slices to squeeze on top.

Chapter 6: Sleep In New York

If you're staying in New York for several days, a week, and longer, you could require rest. The hustle & bustle of a big metropolis can be taxing for people who are used to moving at a slower pace.

The city which never sleeps has lots of places to sleep, since most visitors & even some locals may not realize. Here are some locations to relax in NYC, ranging from budget-friendly rooms to luxury accommodations, contemporary hotspots, and old favorites.

6.1 Atrium of IBM Plaza

New Yorkers flock to this famous public place to soak up the sun and take a break from city's miles of concrete. Since its inception in 1983, the atrium of IBM Plaza has served as a mini-retreat from the metropolis. This indoor space, situated at 590 Madison Avenue, features many tables & chairs for a mid-day sleep.

Bloomingdales is a department store in NYC.

One of Nyc hidden sleep locations is the famed department store. It should be simple to sneak for a nap with so much space and dark corners.

6.2 York, take a nap

Since its inauguration in February 2019, Nap York, NYC leading "nap club," has hosted hundreds of nappers. Monthly memberships at the club range between $35 till $250 monthly. Travelers with layovers at surrounding airports make up the majority of Nap York's clientele.

6.3 Casper's Dreamery is a novel written by Casper.

Dreamery, a prominent mattress business, has taken advantage of its unique product. Nappers receive a 45-min nap, as well as company branded pajamas, sleep masks, a toothbrush, earplugs, & other pre sleep needs, for only $25. Between nappers, all linens are stripped & laundered. The pods are also equipped with innovative ventilation technology, which ensures that they smell fresh & clean.

6.4 The Irving Place Inn

One of Nyc best-kept secrets is this posh hidden gem. The Inn on Irving Place almost like staying at the exclusive club... in the 1800s, with no outward sign. The Inn at Irving Place is indeed a history buff's dream, with 19th-century antiques and advanced technology like flat-screen Televisions & iPhone chargers.

6.5 Hotels in Pods

Pod Hotel is the pinnacle of modern design, and it's a long way away from Of the Inn on Irving Place. The "pod pads" are either completely equipped residences for short-term rent or reasonably priced upmarket hotel rooms. Apartments with one and two bedrooms are available. With the hip, positive structural, and city traveler in mind, these pods are outfitted with contemporary, modern design.

6.6 NEW YOTEL IN NEW YORK

YOTEL is the place to stay if you're a cool techie. This Japanese-inspired resort in the heart of Midtown Manhattan lets you live the good life without a high price tag. This Midtown sanctuary is geared toward tech-savvy guests. YOTEL provides guests with rooms ranging in size from 114 sq ft solitary rooms to a Rooftop King Suite with such a lounge & dining space.

6.7 Meow Parlor is a cat-friendly establishment.

This one is for cat lovers. Meow Parlor is indeed a terrific place to relax & spend time among feline companions, even if it isn't exactly built for sleeping people. When you visit New York City's first cat cafe, no one will blink an eye if you take a short nap with such a kitten.

New York Map

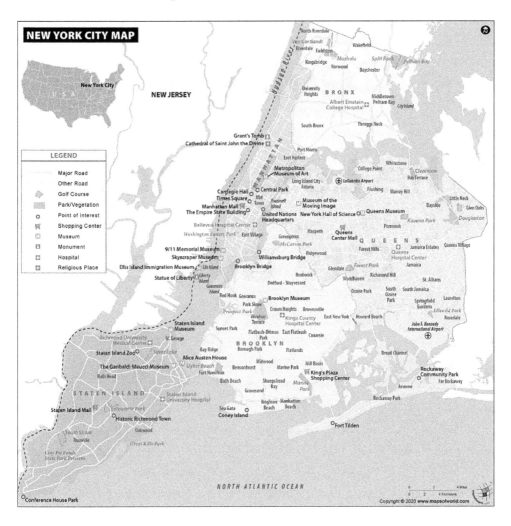

Guide 2

The Los Angeles City Guide

A Guidebook to Explore the Amazing City Of Los Angeles: Best Shops, Bars, Restaurant And Monument.

Introducing Los Angeles:

Los Angeles is the second-most populous city in the United States and is one of the largest in terms of land area. It is the hub of a five-county metro region and is seen as the pattern for the future metropolis—a city at the forefront of all the benefits and drawbacks of major cities. Los Angeles' reputation as a California paradise has been enhanced by the glitz of Hollywood, Beverly Hills, the Sunset Strip, & the world-famous beaches, which have all contributed to the city's extraordinary expansion. Los Angeles is a city of great diversity, with one of the largest Hispanic populations in the U.S., a significant Asian community, and significant communities of people from nearly every ethnic group on the planet. Los Angeles also is a major worldwide commercial and finance hub, as well as a manufacturing and tourism hub. In its huge aggregation of independent and quite diverse neighborhoods, the city has something for everyone:

a sleek, ultra-modern center, miles of magnificent beaches, magnificent mansions and breathtaking canyon residences, and even some of the world's most luxurious shopping and restaurants. However, under the glitz is a struggling, racially divided city with extraordinarily high unemployment rates among young African Americans & Latinos.

Los Angeles, California! Few towns can claim to be so well-known over the world that they are solely known by their initials! L.A. draws tens of millions of people each year & is a must-see for anybody visiting California.

Every day, someone, somewhere, abandon everything in order to pursue his or her "American dream" of being famous and wealthy. Do not be surprised if you see a lot of want-to-be celebs at any time of day or night!

Chapter 1: Experience Los Angeles

Los Angeles is a truly wonderful city, with technicolor sunsets, an incomparably diversified eating scene, and a long history as the world's filmmaking capital.

Los Angeles is unlike any other metropolis on the planet. Every area pulsates with the energy of this bustling global metropolis; world-class performances, magnificent events, and breathtaking natural vistas await you at all hours of the day and night. Read on for unforgettable Los Angeles experiences, from the Historical Core in Downtown L.A. to a famed surf break in Malibu.

Here are some additional ways to immerse yourself in the enchantment of Los Angeles.

1.1 Visit the Venice Boardwalk to see the street performers

The worldwide famous Venice Ocean Front Walk (also known as "Boardwalk") is among the best sites in Los Angeles to watch people, from the colorful locals to tourists from all over the world. At the concrete boardwalk, there's something for everyone: restaurants, specialty shops, and uniquely designed apartments on one side, and artists, street performers, fortune tellers, and more on the other.

1.2 Take in the sights of Los Angeles Phil performs at the Walt Disney Concert Hall

When it first opened to the public on Oct. 22, 2003, Walt Disney Concert Hall had become a Los Angeles landmark. The Los Angeles Philharmonic & the Los Angeles Master Chorale perform at the performance hall, which is situated on Grand Avenue in Downtown L.A. and seats approximately 2,200 people. Walt Disney Concert Hall has gained worldwide critical acclaim and accolades from concertgoers for its spectacular architecture and outstanding sound.

1.3 Visit The Theatre at Ace Hotel and immerse yourself in history

The Ace Hotel in Downtown Los Angeles was erected in 1927 as the United Artists Building on Broadway and 9th Street. C. Howard Crane designed the 13-story structure in the

Spanish Gothic style, based on the Segovia Cathedral in Spain. The United Artists Theatre was the main movie theatre for Charlie Chaplin, Douglas Fairbanks, Mary Pickford, and D.W. Griffith's film business, United Artists. Three stories of the structure house the spectacular 1,600-seat movie theatre.

1.4 Enter Orbit with the Endeavour Space Shuttle

The California Science Center, which opened in February 1998 in Exposition Park, has more than 400,000 square feet and features four major display areas: World of Life, Ecosystems, Creative World, and the Space Shuttle Endeavour. The Science Center also sponsors worldwide touring exhibits such as The Science Behind Pixar & includes a seven-story IMAX Theater dedicated to educational programming.

1.5 Visit the Natural History Museum late at night

The Natural History Institution's (NHM) First Fridays program introduces visitors to the museum and a unique type of museum experience. During these after-hours events, contemporary science, culture, and personal experience collide. First Friday's programs include talks and tours, as well as live performances by artists, bands, and DJs. The museum is also available to the public, featuring pop-up performances & surprises throughout its historic halls and galleries.

1.6 Visit Dodger Stadium to see a game

Los Angeles is the Land of Champions, with some of the world's best sporting arenas. Two Olympiads, NCAA finals, three Super Bowls, NBA and WNBA championships, the World Series, the Stanley Cup, the FIFA World Cup, and more have all been held in Los Angeles venues.

1.7 At Grand Central Market, you can eat your way around the world

The busy Grand Central Market (GCM), which has been a Downtown L.A. fixture since 1917, has lately welcomed a new wave of food & drink merchants. GCM was designated one of the top ten new restaurants in the U.S by Bon Appétit in August 2014. China Cafe, Roast To Go, & Tacos Tumbras. Grand Central Market has 11 of the best latest food and drinks options.

1.8 Cross HOLLYWOOD BOWL OFF YOUR TO-DO LIST

There are few things more distinctively Los Angeles than enjoying a summer evening underneath the stars at the Hollywood Bowl, listening to a performance. The Bowl has welcomed everybody from The Beatles and Lady Gaga, Bob Dylan to Prince and Radiohead, and is one of the most well-known outdoor venues in the world. You haven't truly experienced Los Angeles until you've seen a show in the Hollywood Bowl.

1.9 BREAK ROOM 86: Sing Your Heart Away

Break Room 86 is an '80s-themed karaoke establishment situated in the back of The Queue Hotel in Koreatown, and its part of the Houston Hospitality entertainment collection. It's always a good time with cocktail names that sound like your favorite teen idol & a soundtrack that sounds like your favorite mixtape. Either you're there just for the karaoke or the Atari, sing on stage with a live band or reserve a private room for yourself and & your pals.

1.10 Exchange LA: Dance the Night Out

Exchange LA is a stunning Art Deco tower that's been converted for the modern nightclub experience. It's named after the building's historic hosting of the Los Angeles stock exchange on the Spring Street. Exchange is one of the few prominent clubs in L.A. that routinely books trance D.J.s in contrast to house & techno D.J.s.

1.11 Bring a picnic lunch to Eat|See|Hear

The event, which occurs on Saturday nights at several locations ranging from Downtown Los Angeles to Santa Monica, is free and open to the public. Eat|See|Hear has the West Coast's largest outdoor screen and cutting-edge audio. Every showing includes a carefully prepared menu of food trucks and an introductory performance by a new band.

1.12 Attend the Downtown L.A. Art Walk to meet new artists.

The Downtown L.A. Art Walk occurs on the second Thursday of every month, rain or shine, year-round, with fascinating and unusual offers around every corner. Many of the Downtown Art Walk activities occur between 2nd and 9th Streets, in & around the galleries on Spring and Main Streets. Throughout Downtown L.A., several art-related events, activities, openings, and special programming occur during the Art Walk. Thousands of visitors converge on the region to catch up with friends and take in the local experience as the evening advances. The participating galleries are open from 12 p.m. until 10 p.m. Details can be found in the individual gallery listings.

1.13 Jazz at LACMA: Get in the Mood

Over one hundred concerts are presented yearly by the award-winning Department of Music Programs at the Los Angeles County Museum of Art (LACMA), showcasing prominent international and local ensembles in classical, jazz, Latin, and new music programs. Jazz at LACMA has previously featured giants, including Wayne Shorter, Kenny Burrell, John Clayton, Arturo Sandoval, Les McCann, Billy Childs, Cannonball-Coltrane Project, and Ernie Watts, and is one of the museum's most popular events.

1.14 Discover the fabled Sunset Strip.

Sunset Boulevard is among the most recognized streets in Los Angeles, and the iconic Sunset Strip, which extends 1.5 miles from West Hollywood to Beverly Hills, is possibly its most recognized segment. Book a room at the historic Chateau Marmont or a modern hotel such as the Andaz West Hollywood, the Mondrian, or the London West Hollywood. The Whisky a Go-Go, The Roxy, and the Viper Room are still running great, but newer places like Eveleigh, the Church Key, and BOA Steakhouse draw both tourists and residents. Bar Marmont, Skybar, and the Comedy Store are among the nightlife options.

Chapter 2: Los Angeles Tour

Whether you're a first-time tourist to Los Angeles or a lifelong Angeleno, the City of Angels always has something fresh to offer. There are tours available to help you experience L.A. that serve a wide range of budgets and interests. Read on to learn more about Los Angeles tours, including museum and gastronomy excursions to eco-friendly biking and breathtaking helicopter and boat experiences.

2.1 Tour Hollywood at Warner Bros. Studio

The Warner Bros. Studios VIP Tour provides a unique and intimate look into the workings of Hollywood. An interesting two-hour tour takes groups of 12 people across backlot streets, soundstages, sets, & craft shops. There are no two tours alike. Visitors can take a tour of a popular television show's set, watch Foley artists make audio effects for movies, learn how sets are built, explore millions of props, and much more.

2.2 Universal Studios Hollywood Tour

One of Universal Studios Hollywood's must-see attractions is the renowned Studio Tour. The Studio Tour, narrated by Jimmy Fallon, allows visitors to tour the functioning backlot of a real Hollywood film studio. The tram journey brings passengers past sets from films such as "Psycho," "War of the Worlds," "Jaws," & others, as well as some blazing special effects. The tour also includes the world's largest 3-D experience, filmmaker Peter Jackson's heart-pounding King Kong 360 3-D.

2.3 The Art Muse Los Angeles Tour

Art Muse Los Angeles is a group of art historians, artists, and educators who provide private museum visits in Los Angeles. These art experts and enthusiasts provide talks to small groups of people ranging from beginners to collectors and connoisseurs, customizing their presentations for each type of visitor. Many of L.A.'s main institutions, such as the Getty Center, Norton Simon Museum, Hammer Museum, Los Angeles County Museum of Art, and Museum of Contemporary Art, provide tours through Art Muse. Art Muse also organizes tours of the seasonal art fairs & select contemporary art galleries in Los Angeles. Downtown Los Angeles, the Wilshire Corridor, Culver City, and Bergamot

Station are among the districts where gallery tours are offered.

2.4 Hikes and Bikes Los Angeles

Book a Bikes and Hikes LA trip for an eco-friendly, healthy manner to see Los Angeles. These tours are geared for everyone from avid bikers & hikers to beginners and the casual biker/hiker. "L.A. In a Day," a 32-mile, 5-hour excursion, is the most popular trip. The excursions begin in West Hollywood and travel through opulent Beverly Hills and Bel-Air, as well as L.A.'s world-famous beach towns of Santa Monica, Venice, and Marina Del Rey, as well as the historical movie studios of Culver City. Bikes and Hikes LA, which specializes in individual day trips, also offers group trip alternatives for friends and families, corporate clients, social organizations, incentive travel, and school and university groups.

2.5 Catalin Express

Book a Bikes and Hikes LA trip for an eco-friendly, healthy manner to see Los Angeles. These tours are geared for everyone from avid bikers & hikers to beginners and the casual biker/hiker. "L.A. In a Day," a 32-mile, 5-hour excursion, is the most popular trip. The excursions begin in West Hollywood and travel through wealthy Beverly Hills and Bel-Air and L.A.'s world-famous beach towns of Santa Monica, Venice, and Marina Del Rey, as well as the historical movie studios of Culver City. Bikes and Hikes LA, specializing in individual day trips, also offers group trip alternatives for friends and families, corporate clients, social organizations, incentive travel, and school and university groups.

2.6 Club Crawl Tour Los Angeles

Hollywood Club Crawl leads you on a nightlife tour of 4 Hollywood clubs every Friday and Saturday, with VIP entrance and no cover charges or lineups. Come by yourself, with a date, or with a group for a great night in Hollywood. At 10 p.m., guests gather at the St. Felix on Cahuenga Boulevard. You'll be introduced to your hosts at check-in, given your Club Crawl wristbands, & directed to the bar for exclusive drink specials. For the full night, pre-sale tickets are $25. Cash tickets are available for $30 at the event check-in desk, but only if the event is not sold out.

2.7 Los Angeles Orbic Air Helicopter Tour

Orbic Air has been one of Southern California's finest helicopter companies for over 20 years, providing Los Angeles helicopter charters, Hollywood helicopter tours, helicopter training, aerial photography, production, and helicopter leasing. Orbic Air is located at Van Nuys Airport, centrally positioned in Los Angeles, with easy access to Hollywood, Malibu, and Santa Monica. L.A. LIVE, Hollywood and the Pacific coast are among the many helicopter tour destinations, as are landing packages like the Romance Package and the Shoreline Picnic.

2.8 Hollywood/Tourcouch Charter & Tours by Starline Tours

Starline Tours has been providing guests from worldwide with the best of Los Angeles since 1935, when it first introduced the Movie Stars Homes Tour. The Grand City Tour, the LGBT itinerary, and one-hour Hollywood Fun Trips are just a few of the sightseeing tours offered by Starline. There are also private bus charters available.

2.9 Sunset Ranch Hollywood Los Angeles

Get in the saddles with Sunset Ranch Hollywood, the only horse ranch in greater Los Angeles, for a unique tour of Griffith Park. Sunset Ranch offers guided trail rides, boarding, and instruction, among other services and activities. The Hollywood Sign is seen from the one trail ride through Griffith Park. The trip to the top of Griffith Park takes two hours and offers a breathtaking panoramic view of Los Angeles. Lunch Ride, BBQ Ride, Sunset Dinner Ride, and Kids' Party are among the additional ride options available.

Chapter 3: Shop Los Angeles

With its movie-star glamour, wide beaches, and legendary nightlife, Los Angeles attracts visitors. The Los Angeles shopping environment, on the other hand, is just as appealing, with everything from designer apparel to electronics & artisan delicacies.

3.1 Rodeo Drive Los Angeles

A stroll down Rodeo Drive in Beverly Hills is a must; the walkways are lined with some of the world's most luxurious and exclusive stores. Armani, Christian Dior, Coco Chanel, and Gucci are just a few well-known fashion houses with outlets here. You can't afford anything if you have to ask what it really costs. However, gawking at the high-end window displays—or the affluent and famous walking their pedigreed canines or driving Lamborghinis along this famed street—is free of charge.

3.2 Farmers Market Los Angeles

Don't miss a stroll around the Farmers Market's shops and stalls on Fairfax Avenue & West Third Street, where produce, as well as other foodstuffs, seem to be crammed into every available area. (There's even a bakery for dogs!) Movie stars and studio executives may be seen grabbing some quick power breakfast. Walt Disney is said to have sat at a table while designing Disneyland. It may be clogged with tourists by the busload, but it's still a wonderful spot to visit.

3.3 Abbot Kenney Boulevard Los Angeles

Abbot Kinney Boulevard in Venice is the place to go for fashionable, unique treasures like vintage apparel and local art.

3.4 Melrose Avenue Los Angeles

Melrose Avenue is where avant-garde clothes, tacky presents, home décor, and pop art may be found. For antique and designer clothing, go to Wasteland, or for art deco design, go to Thanks for the Memories. On Melrose Avenue, celebrities are common; for the best chance of seeing one, visit a busy Saturday and sit outside one of the coffee shops or eateries.

3.5 Montana Avenue Los Angeles

Montana Avenue in Santa Monica is the place to go for breezy, affluent luxury. Designer apparel and home furnishings abound in unique boutiques and galleries; when you need a break, try a yoga class or visit a spa.

3.6 The Groove Los Angeles

The Grove is an outdoor Los Angeles mall surrounded by a beautifully groomed grassy field with a fountain that moves to music on the hour, and it seems like an imagined small town. Take the free electric trolley, which harkens back to a more opulent past, for a leisurely tour of the businesses. Parking is normally ample, but it might not be easy to find on Friday and Saturday nights.

3.7 Citadel Outlets Los Angeles

Only in Los Angeles will you find a former factory that resembles an Assyrian palace and now is home to Calvin Klein, Levi's, Guess, Converse, and other outlet stores. Check for an information booth at Citadel Outlets and inquire about any special promotions that may be offered.

Chapter 4: Entertainment in Los Angeles

The entertainment options in Los Angeles are limitless. A night out in Los Angeles, on the other hand, does not necessitate hundreds of dollars in bottle service. For less than $20, you can enjoy some of L.A.'s most exciting entertainment & nightlife.

4.1 Mayan Theatre Los Angeles

On Friday nights, the Mayan plays a hip-hop, mix of salsa, and house music for a $12 cover charge for all night, or you may sign up for the mayan guest list via their website & get in for free before 10:30 p.m.

4.2 Casey's Irish Pub Los Angeles

On Sunday and Monday nights, Casey's Irish Pub offers all-day happy hour with PBR and pub fries.

4.3 TCL Chinese Theatre IMAX Los Angeles

The legendary TCL Chinese Theatre is the best venue to view a movie in Los Angeles and don't be hesitant with putting your feet and hands in the cement outside.

4.4 The Airliner Los Angeles

Low-End Theory, the famed monthly electronic music showcase that just concluded its 12-year run & launched the careers of musicians like Nosaj Thing and Flying Lotus was held at The Airliner and is still one of L.A.'s best-kept secrets.

4.5 The Satellite Los Angeles

The Satellite is the spot to go if you're looking for up & coming indie bands. Play a game of pool in their back room if you're not enjoying the band on stage.

4.6 The Roxy Los Angeles

There's no better spot to hear raw, unadulterated rock-and-roll than West Hollywood's Sunset Strip. Whenever you visit the Roxy, you won't have to break the bank to have a good time. On the Roxy, the small upstairs bar features a range of intimate concerts for less than $10.

4.7 The Pub at the Golden Road Los Angeles

Beer does not seem to be nasty just because it's cheap. With 20 rotating taps, the Pub at Golden Road Brewing is the place to go for artisan beer. Do Munch on their house made vegan Bavarian pretzel after a pint or two.

4.8 Universal City Walk-Howl at the Moon Los Angeles

Visit Howl at the Moon, a dueling piano bar on Universal City Walk, for a night out. Enjoy three drinks only for the price of one on Sundays.

4.9 McCabe's Guitar Shop Los Angeles

McCabe's Guitar Shop in Santa Monica offers live music in a unique setting. The majority of concerts are under $20.

4.10 The Ice House Los Angeles

Every Thursday at The Ice House in Pasadena, there is a show called Stand Up All-Stars, which features up-and-comers as well as local stalwarts like Adam Carolla. General Admission tickets are $15, while VIP tickets are $20 and feature front-of-line access and preferred seats.

4.11 Bigfoot West Los Angeles

You don't really have to be the next Mariah Carey to have a good time at Bigfoot West's karaoke night. This Westside favorite has a distinctive atmosphere because of the log cabin atmosphere.

Chapter 5: Eating in Los Angeles

Whether you like to rub elbows with the celebrities at cutting-edge eateries or eat West Coast classics at a vintage diner, trendy Los Angeles has you covered. Eating healthily has never been easier; being the epicenter of a health-conscious lifestyle, LA is home to a plethora of juice bars, vegan-friendly eateries, and organic farmers' markets that will satisfy even the most health-conscious diners.

Here is the list of foods that Los Angeles excels at more than anywhere else in the United States, along with only a few local examples to illustrate the point.

5.1 Fries and burger

This would be a sin to visit Los Angeles without sampling a delicious cheeseburger & fries from In-N-Out Burger, the state's cult burger restaurant. If you order your meal "animal style," a famous "secret menu" euphemism for a substantial topping of melted cheese, Thousand Island dressing, and grilled onions, you'll get bonus points.

Places to try: In-N-Out Burger is a must-try (Apple Pan, Capitol Burger, and Pie N' Burger)

5.2 Sushi

It's no surprise that Los Angeles is famed for its wonderful sushi offerings, with an entire section named "Little Tokyo." Many of LA's high-profile celebs frequent Nobu, which is owned by celebrity chef Nobu (you're likely to see a Kardashian), while Sugarfish, a popular local restaurant, is known for traditional high-quality sushi.

Places to try: Try Nobu (903 La Cienega Boulevard) or Sugarfish in the Little Tokyo neighborhood (various locations)

5.3 Hot Dogs

Hot dogs are a North American favorite that is best eaten from the inside of a baseball stadium. The simple hot dog has been elevated to a whole new level in Los Angeles, with fast food places all over the city delivering their own distinct and scrumptious twist on the American classic.

Places to try: Pink's Hot Dogs (709 North La Brea Avenue) is just a vintage roadside stand known for its chili cheese dog, a frankfurter topped with beef chili, melted cheese, and onions.

5.4 Sandwich with a French dip

The delectable sandwich has its origins in Southern California and is said to have been created by accident by restaurant owner Philippe Mathieu in 1918. Meat is placed in a gravy-dipped French bread, topped with cheese, and served with a selection of sides in this mouthwatering dinner.

Places to try: Philippe The Original is a good place to start (1001 North Alameda)

5.5 Mexican cuisine

It's no secret that LA has some of the best Mexican cuisines in the country, whether it's fresh burritos from the taco truck or chargrilled carne asada from a dine-in restaurant.

Places to try: Broken Spanish offers an elegant and sophisticated twist on Mexican cuisine (1050 South Flower Street). El Chato Taco Truck sells inexpensive, delectable street tacos (5300 West Olympic Boulevard).

5.6 Parmigiana chicken

This dish consists of a breaded chicken breast which is coated in a thick tomato sauce and afterward topped with a variety of cheeses such as parmesan, mozzarella, and provolone.

Places to try: Dan Tana's (9071 Santa Monica Boulevard), a cozy eatery that has been serving up a classic rendition on the famous chicken parm since 1964.

5.7 Toast with Ricotta

Sqirl's ricotta toast has gone viral on Instagram and has become an online legend. People queue outside this unusual cafe to try their thickly sliced brioche toast smeared in homemade ricotta & topped with a variety of colorful jams - a truly delectable way to start the day.

Places to try: Sqirl (720 Virgil Avenue #4) is a good place to start.

5.8 Apple Pie

Dessert lovers need not fear in Los Angeles, which is recognized for its abundance of healthful cafes. The city has some of the greatest spots to try this traditional American delicacy, with many old-school diners & modern pie shops.

Places to try: Jones Hollywood (7205 California State Route 2) is known for having the best apple pie in town. Since 1947, The Apple Pan (10801 West Pico Boulevard) has served the meal at its typical diner counter.

5.9 Wine

California's official drink is wine, and the state produces some of the best in the world. If you don't want to drive all the way to the vineyards of Napa Valley or the Orange

County, you may taste the delectable drink at one of LA's lovely wineries.

Places to try: Malibu Wine Safari (32111 Mulholland Highway) offers scenic views, local wine tastings, or travel downtown for sampling at San Antonio Winery (737 Lamar Street).

Chapter 6: Stay in Los Angeles

Los Angeles is a whirlwind of roads, sleazy suburbs, coastline, high-gloss neighborhoods, & the extreme lifestyles, all surrounded by the sandy beaches & snowcapped mountains soaring above 10,000 feet. Because the region you choose to stay in could have a massive effect on the trip, we've put together a list of the best places to stay within Los Angeles.

6.1 Places to stay in Downtown

Downtown Los Angeles, the city's historic hub, has undergone a revival. Apartments have been converted from elegant historical banks and the hotels. LA Live, a $2.5 billion of shopping & entertainment complex, has brought the cinemas, high-end hotels, a variety of restaurants, and nightclubs to the area.

However, it is still a diverse neighborhood, with adobe structures & skid row (one of the greatest concentrations of the homeless persons in the United States), Mexican market stalls, avant-garde art galleries, & high-rise of corporate towers all within a few blocks.

There is a wide range of accommodations available, from simple beds to opulent hotels. However, though Downtown is a center of the MTA's networks & public transportation, getting to the beaches isn't easy.

1. **Ace Hotel is the best place to stay in Los Angeles if you want a cool Los Angeles style:** This modern hotel in the middle of Downtown provides clean, trendy rooms and the rooftop pool.

2. **Los Angeles Athletics Club is a sports club based in Los Angeles:** The top 3 floors of the private clubhouse a hotel with around 72 tastefully decorated rooms; the real advantage is a complimentary access to the club's gym, whirlpool, & sauna.

6.2 Places to Stay in the Hollywood

Hollywood has lured millions of visitors, and the equal number of the hopefuls enticed by the potential of riches & glory since movies & their stars emerged international emblems of the good life.

With the creation of the new tourist plaza & shopping malls in recent years, things have lightened up. Today, corporate hype, Hollywood's contradictory elements of freshly polished nostalgia, & deep set seediness make it one of LA's most diverse neighborhoods – and among the greatest sites for the bar-hopping & clubbing.

1. **Hollywood Bed and Breakfast is the best place to stay for a unique experience.** This B & B is housed in 1912 mansion that seems like it belongs from Dr Seuss book. With 4 cozy rooms & a little pool, it's close to everything.

2. **Magic Castle Hotel is the best choice for the modern simplicity.** A popular hotel featuring clean, modern rooms & suites, as well as a heated pool & free drink, sweets, and cookies available 24 hours in a day.

6.3 Places to Stay in West LA

The so-called "Westside" of Los Angeles begins just beyond Hollywood in West LA, home to some of the city's most affluent neighborhoods.

The restaurants & boutiques of West Hollywood & Beverly Hills and the magnificent Getty Center, perched high above the Los Angeles basin, are highlights.

1. **Farmer's Daughter is the best for Midwestern kitsch:** This attractive boutique establishment with aspects of "country fashioned" Midwestern kitsch is located right next to (naturally) the Farmers' Market.

2. **Bel-Air is the best place to go for unfettered luxury:** Constructed in 1946 and now managed by the Sultan of Brunei,

LA's most opulent hotel is set in a lushly vegetated canyon and designed as an Arabian oasis.

3. **Beverly Hills is the best place for celebrity-like living:** This luxurious hotel on Sunset Boulevard, dubbed "The Pink Palace," has a full-service La Prairie Spa as well as a lovely outdoor pool.

6.4 Places to Stay in Santa Monica, Malibu & Venice

1. **Ambrose is the best option for a beach bed:** With Arts & Crafts-style decor & boutique accommodations, this is the greatest option for inland Santa Monica.

2. **Channel Road Inn is ideal for a romantic break:** The B&B rooms here are set in lower Santa Monica Canyon (northwest of Santa Monica) and provide beach views, a hot tub, and complimentary bike rentals.

3. **The Kinney is the best place to visit in Venice Beach:** This stylish California hotel is just 0.9 miles from Venice Beach and features bicycle rentals, an outside area with such a fire pit, an outdoor heated pool, and ping pong tables.

6.5 Places to Stay in South Bay

1. **The Beach House is the best place to stay if you want to be pampered to the max:** Fireplaces, balconies, wet bars, hot tubs, stereos, and refrigerators are all available in the two-room suites. Many of the accommodations have views of the ocean.

2. **Portofino Hotel & Yacht Club has the best views of the sea:** The top suites of this oceanfront suite hotel include hot tubs and beautiful views of King Harbor's affluent playground.

6.6 Places to Stay in Orange country

1. **Huntington Surf Inn is the best place to stay in town if you want to go surfing**: With nine modest but incredibly cool rooms with a pop-art decor centered on Southern California beach & surfing culture, the hotel is right on the beach and near to the pier. Many professional surfers choose to reside here.

2. **The Ritz-Carlton Laguna Niguel is the best place to stay if you want to be near the water**: This beautiful Ritz-Carlton is possibly the best in town due to its gorgeous oceanfront location. The rooms and suites are lavishly appointed.

Los Angeles Map

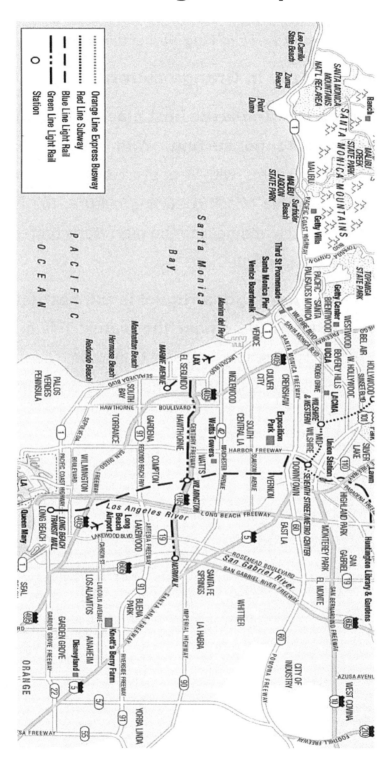

Lightning Source UK Ltd.
Milton Keynes UK
UKHW031453211222
414213UK00010B/730